Young Brer Rabbit

and Other Trickster Tales from the Americas

collected and adapted by
JAQUELINE SHACHTER WEISS

Illustrated by
CLINTON ARROWOOD

STEMMER
HOUSE
PUBLISHERS, INC.

OWINGS MILLS, MARYLAND

Inquiries should be directed to
Stemmer House Publishers, Inc.
2627 Caves Road
Owings Mills, Maryland 21117

A Barbara Holdridge book

Printed and bound in Hong Kong
Second Edition 1986

gr. 3-4

Library of Congress Cataloging in Publication Data

Weiss, Jaqueline Shachter.
   Young Brer Rabbit, and other trickster tales from the Americas.

   "A Barbara Holdridge book."
   Summary: A collection of fifteen Brer Rabbit trickster tales from the Afro-American culture of Central and South America and the Caribbean.
   1. Tales—Central America.   2. Tales—South America.
3. Animals—Folklore. 4. Rabbits—Folklore. [1. Folklore—Central America.   2. Folklore—South America]
I. Arrowood, Clinton, ill.   II. Title.   III. Title:
Young Brer Rabbit.
PZ8.1.1W4835Yo   1985   398.2′45   84-26889
ISBN 0-88045-138-6

Contents

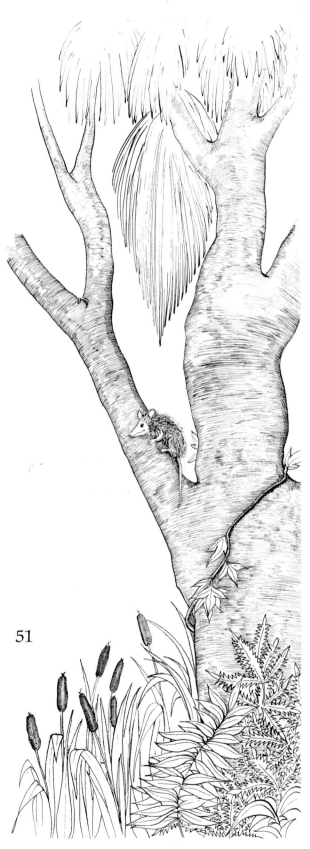

With love to my husband, George,
and my children, Sherry, Ross, Scott and Steve

Foreword

Young Brer Rabbit and Other Trickster Tales from the Americas is a fine example of the manner in which an oral tradition can spread over a large area. In the process, some things remain firmly the same (the trickiness of the rabbit and the gullibility of the other animals) while others change, probably to suit the temperament of the storytellers as much as to record differences in environment. It is quite extraordinary that this rich African lore managed to penetrate into the four major languages used in the Americas, (French, English, Portuguese and Spanish), and to stay alive in all, even up to today. Jaqueline Shachter Weiss has collected and retold stories from all four of these languages in an easy style full of down-to-earth humor. What storyteller could resist learning "The Moon" so as to be able to call out that impudent ending! And the actions of "Weeds" are enough to set a whole audience scratching and laughing. But most important, the collection demonstrates that in at least a few tales, we have a common cultural heritage with many diverse peoples of the Americas.

January 1985

Anne Pellowski
Former Director-Librarian
Information Center on Children's Cultures,
A Service of the United States Committee for
UNICEF

Introduction

Brer Rabbit tales have been with us a long time. They were shared by proud African people who were brought to the Americas as slaves. Later, others recorded the stories. They were told not only in the United States, but also in Brazil, Panama, Venezuela, Colombia and the Caribbean islands.

In the African folk tales, small animals, such as the turtle or praying mantis, were praised for what they did well. As an example, the turtle was "slow but sure." For millions of people who spoke a Bantu language in central, eastern and southern Africa, the rabbit was the story hero. He was "small but clever and brave."

Among the Ashanti of West Africa, the hero was the spider, Anansi. He was "small but tricky." (*Anansi* means "spider" in their Akan language.) Though Anansi is a well-known folk character in Guyana, Jamaica and the Virgin Islands, the rabbit is appreciated more in most of the Americas.

Brer Rabbit is a shortened form of "Brother Rabbit." ("Brer" may be spelled "Br'er." There are slightly different forms in some Caribbean islands.) Brer Rabbit is his name in most English-speaking lands. In Venezuela, where he is especially popular today, as well as in Colombia and Panama, he is called *Tío Conejo* ("Uncle Rabbit"). In Cuba, he is *Hermano Rabito* ("Brother Rabbit") and in Brazil, *o coelho* ("the rabbit"). He will be called "Brer Rabbit" throughout these stories.

The slaves, made to feel small and weak, were comforted by Brer

3

Rabbit. They told stories about him to teach other slaves to be as clever as this tiny animal. Through their folk hero, they showed their wit to a doubting world.

The African storytellers who were captured and brought to the Americas were people living close to nature. They thought *all* animals—including men and women—are related, because they are the works of the Creator. Since the animals are members of one big family, they are called "Brer" and "Sis," "Pa" and "Ma," "Uncle" and "Aunt," "Godfather" and "Godmother," "Brer Grandfather" and "Sis Grandmother." Even the Creator is in the family as "Father God."

The talking animals act like people most of the time. There are surprises, however. In "The Fair Judge," from Colombia, and "The Wind Storm," from Puerto Rico, beasts that are helped turn against their helper and try to kill him. This "law of the jungle" shows true-to-life themes in amusing stories.

Brer Rabbit outsmarts such big animals as Sis Jaguar in Brazil and Brer Tiger almost everywhere else in Latin America. These two strong animals may, in truth, be one and the same in folk tales. The jaguar is a native American cat; the tiger is not. In most of the Americas, though, the jaguar is more often called "tiger."

In the tales from Brazil, the animals have a queen, Sis Jaguar, and sometimes a king. There is no clear reason why this is true only in Brazil. In other lands, there is only a King of the Beasts.

Brer Lion and Brer Elephant are African beasts that appear in several tales. Other local animals, plants and customs mentioned in the stories reflect their American setting. While a Venezuelan story appropriately takes place in the Andes Mountains, fishing and the beach are important in an island tale.

Similar Brer Rabbit tales have been told in more than one country. Over a period of a hundred years, changes have been made to suit the location. Among the stories with the same main idea are "The Wax Doll" from Colombia and "The Wonderful Tar-Baby Story" from the United States. "The Wax Doll" struck the writer as being more amusing.

The stories in this book are from the Spanish, Portuguese and French languages. The sources of the story ideas are listed in the bibliography. Many tales presented here have not been retold in English before. Some are published for the first time. Since Brer Rabbit tales from the United States have already been published in English, they are not included.

It is hoped that readers who have a sense of humor will be amused at the pattern in many of the stories and each one's fitting ending. May you enjoy the wit and repeated tricks that have made Brer Rabbit famous!

Norristown, Pennsylvania   J. S. W.
February 1985

Young Brer Rabbit

Young Brer Rabbit

WHEN BRER RABBIT WAS VERY YOUNG, his mother, Ma Rabbit, would warn him, "Look out for Brer Tiger! He eats small animals!" The young rabbit heard so much about Brer Tiger that he thought his enemy must be a giant, even taller than the tallest tree.

One day, Ma Rabbit and her son were walking through the rain forest looking for food. When they peeked through some bushes, they saw an animal with silky yellow fur and black markings. Little Brer Rabbit spotted him first and shouted, "Ma, let's go closer to see him better."

Ma Rabbit was afraid. She grabbed her son and quickly ran home. "That's Brer Tiger!" she said, catching her breath. "If he sees us, we'll be his dinner!"

But to Brer Rabbit, the enemy seemed not the least bit frightening. The little fellow just could not believe that the handsome yellow and black animal was the same beast Ma Rabbit feared.

Some time later, young Brer Rabbit was alone when he faced Brer Tiger. His enemy had a gun swinging from his right shoulder.

Brer Tiger saw the young cottontail. "You must be little Brer Rabbit. I've wanted to meet you," he said in a friendly voice.

Brer Rabbit was polite but did not move. "Excuse me, Brer Tiger, I can't stop to chat," he replied. "My mother is waiting for me at home."

"Ah, I know Ma Rabbit doesn't like me," Brer Tiger said sadly.

"It's not that, Brer Tiger, it's . . ." Brer Rabbit changed the subject when he saw the shiny gun. "What's that, Brer Tiger?"

Brer Tiger smiled. "My son, this is a gun given to me by a friend who's a hunter. My friend let me have it only because I've done so much for him. I use it to scare my enemies."

Brer Rabbit thought, "How I would like to find a friend who'd give me a gun! I could hunt all day in the mountains."

Now the only reason Brer Tiger was friendly was that he had just enjoyed a big meal. Any other time he would have gobbled Brer Rabbit without talking to him. But the beast could not eat another bite. He wanted to keep Brer Rabbit around until he was hungry again.

"You might like to hunt," Brer Tiger said. "It's good to learn by aiming at flies, mosquitoes and fleas. How would you like to go to the country of the fleas to hunt?"

"I'd love to, Brer Tiger!" shouted little Brer Rabbit. He didn't know that there was no such country.

The two animals went down the road. A few moments later, Brer Tiger said, "Let's bet, Brer Rabbit, to see who can hunt more fleas. For each flea I kill, I'll have the right to bite you. For each one you kill, you can bite me."

"Okay," said trusting Brer Rabbit.

Luckily, Brer Bee was close enough to hear the bet. He whispered into one of Brer Rabbit's long ears, "Don't be a fool, Brer Rabbit. As soon as Brer Tiger bites you, he'll eat you! I'll help you, but you must do what I say." Brer Bee told him his plan before he flew away.

After Brer Rabbit walked a while with Brer Tiger, he asked, "Is the gun loaded?"

"Of course it is," Brer Tiger answered. "It has five bullets."

Brer Rabbit said, "I'd like to try your gun now, but I don't know how it works."

Brer Tiger showed him how to use it. Then Brer Rabbit aimed carefully at something far away. "I'm going to shoot a fly over there, Brer Tiger," he said.

"Where? I don't see it," Brer Tiger replied, "not even if I strain my eyes."

"It's stinging the nose of a brown horse who's standing about two miles from here," Brer Rabbit told him.

"How can you see that far?" Brer Tiger asked. "Did you kill the fly?"

"I think so. I'm almost sure," Brer Rabbit answered. "Let's find the horse to see for ourselves." They walked over two miles while Brer Bee flew ahead and told the horse what to say.

When they finally arrived, Brer Rabbit said, "Brer Horse, I

fired a shot at a fly that was bothering you. Do you remember the fly?"

"Yes, a while ago, it was on my nose. The pest was struck by a bullet that almost hit my head!" Brer Horse complained.

Brer Tiger had to praise Brer Rabbit's aim, but he was getting

hungry. He said, "Let's hurry to the land of the fleas." He licked his lips as he thought, "I'll eat him at the turn in the road."

Brer Rabbit stopped to look carefully all over Brer Tiger.

"What's wrong?" Brer Tiger asked.

"Nothing, just don't move," Brer Rabbit shouted. "We don't have to go to the land of the fleas. Your fur is full of fleas. I'm going to kill them, one by one!"

Brer Tiger was afraid of anyone who could shoot a fly two miles away. The big beast took three jumps into the bushes and was out of sight.

Brer Rabbit carried the gun home to his mother. When Ma Rabbit saw it, she cried with fright and wiped her eyes on the hem of her dress. Her moans stopped only when her son hugged her and said solemnly, "You're right, Ma. We have to be on guard always against Brer Tiger!"

The Root

ONE COOL MORNING, BRER RABBIT sniffed the refreshing air of the Andes Mountains. He had been leading Brer Tiger on a merry chase, and now he enjoyed resting on a bed of moss beside a waterfall. Just then, Brer Rabbit saw his enemy fall into a pond. When Brer Tiger got out covered with mud, Brer Rabbit laughed and laughed.

One of his forest friends heard him. It was lazy Brer Weasel, whose nap was disturbed. "What's funny, Brer Rabbit?" he asked.

"Ha, ha! Muddy Brer Tiger looked so silly. You should have seen him!" Brer Rabbit giggled as he spoke.

"Hmmm," murmured Brer Weasel. "Sooner or later, he may laugh at *you*."

Brer Rabbit had more to say, but the sleepy weasel grunted, "Uh! Please let me sleep. I'm very tired, you know."

After Brer Rabbit left, Brer Weasel opened one eye long enough to be sure he was gone. Then Brer Weasel rolled himself into a ball and kept on sleeping. He got up when Brer Tiger poked him in the ribs. "Ugh," Brer Weasel said as he yawned. "Are you looking for Brer Rabbit?" he asked.

Brer Tiger nodded. "I'll make Brer Rabbit pay for the way he's treated me," he said.

Brer Weasel wanted to get on the good side of Brer Tiger. The weasel asked, "If I tell you where Brer Rabbit went, what will you give me?"

Brer Tiger's wild eyes glowed. "Don't worry, you'll get something," he roared. "Now tell me where he is."

Thanks to Brer Weasel's help, Brer Tiger found Brer Rabbit in the valley and chased him. With each leap, he got closer.

Gasping, Brer Rabbit took a chance. He threw stones ahead of him, hoping Brer Tiger would follow them. He himself went the other way in back of a tree. He hid among the tree's thick roots on the damp ground. When he felt like sneezing, he held his breath and prayed that Brer Tiger would not find him.

Brer Tiger saw everything his enemy did. The angry beast tiptoed toward the little one. When he got to the tree, Brer Tiger silently leaned against it. Brer Tiger slowly brought his arm toward the other side of the tree and grabbed Brer Rabbit.

When he felt Brer Tiger's claws on him, poor Brer Rabbit quickly had to test his luck. He cried, "You wanted to catch me, but you only got the tree's root!"

Brer Tiger thought he truly had only the root, so he let go. Now free, Brer Rabbit hopped away as fast as he could. When Brer Tiger looked behind the tree, Brer Rabbit was gone. "I've lost him again!" the tiger growled as he retraced his steps through the forest.

Brer Weasel saw Brer Tiger return. He shouted, "Brer Tiger! Brer Tiger! Give me what you promised!" Brer Weasel climbed down the tree for his gift.

"Here you are!" the beast roared. Brer Tiger threw Brer Weasel by his tail high in the air. He landed far away with the seat of his pants on a thorn bush.

Brer Weasel was shocked and disappointed. He grumbled, "Thorns in my seat are not the kind of reward I expected. I'll never help Brer Tiger again!" Then he dragged himself into the forest, moaning as he pulled out each painful thorn.

Young Anteater

HUNGRY BRER TIGER AND BRER FOX often thought of eating the children of Pa and Ma Anteater. All of the children were fast on their feet except the youngest, who was small and weak. He never wanted to eat, so he became ugly. His hair was short and his claws were always broken.

Once, Brer Tiger and Brer Fox were chasing the anteater children. All of them got away except the weak brother. He tried to escape by going in circles until he came to the edge of a hill. There he stopped short, afraid. He began to cry, "Oh, no! Brer Tiger and Brer Fox are going to eat me!"

Brer Rabbit, a stranger to the anteater, heard his cries. He said, "Just do what I do. I can save you." Brer Rabbit curled himself into a ball and rolled down the hill. The little anteater did the same, and so Brer Fox and Brer Tiger left him alone.

The little anteater shouted to his friend, "Thank you for saving my life!" His family never knew about his narrow escape, though he was breathless when he went home.

That night, everyone enjoyed Ma Anteater's dinner except the ugly anteater, who hardly put a fork to his mouth. At the table, Ma Anteater told her children stories about a living hero, Brer

Rabbit, a more clever creature than big Brer Tiger. Her child with the broken claws decided to learn from this hero.

At sunrise the next day, the little anteater left to see Brer Rabbit, his new friend. Meanwhile, Brer Tiger was looking for the ugly anteater, to be his breakfast. "Do you know where Ma Anteater's child has gone?" Brer Tiger asked. He was talking to Brer Monkey, who had seen everything from his treetop home.

"What a sleepyhead you are!" Brer Monkey told him. "He went to Brer Rabbit's place early while you were still in bed. He said he might stay a while."

That day and for some time afterwards, Brer Tiger watched outside Brer Rabbit's hole. Of course, he was waiting for the little anteater.

On the inside, Brer Rabbit took a good look at the weak anteater. Then the rabbit shook his head, rubbed his chin, and asked, "Will you accept the help you really need?"

"Yes," the little anteater agreed. "Please tell me how you fool Brer Tiger."

Brer Rabbit had never been admired before. He was flattered, but he was too shy to show it. He changed the subject to ask, "Why do you have such broken claws?"

"My mother says I'm not healthy 'cause I don't eat well," the little anteater explained.

"If you want to escape Brer Tiger," Brer Rabbit told him, "you must be strong."

"But I can't stand food," the little anteater said, wrinkling his nose at the thought.

At this point, Brer Rabbit served ice cream. The little anteater ate a spoonful. "Um, that's good," he shouted, smacking his lips. "Please give me more!"

The little anteater stayed many days with Brer Rabbit and learned to enjoy eating. When he left, he was heavy, strong and handsome. His chubbiness surprised Brer Tiger, who had been watching outside Brer Rabbit's home for the young anteater. "Now that he's fat," Brer Tiger thought, "he'll make a better meal. He'll also be slower and easier to catch."

Brer Tiger jumped in front of the young anteater. Surprised, the now-strong anteater rose on his hind legs. He dared Brer Tiger, "Come on and fight! I'm not the weak fool I used to be. Come closer!"

Brer Tiger looked at the sharp claws and powerful arms of the young anteater. "I need help," he said as he left, returning later with Brer Fox.

The young anteater was ready for them with his long, sharp snout, sticky tongue and great hairy tail. He looked straight at them and put on a show. First, he went to a big banana plant and uprooted it easily. Next, he surprised his enemies by squeezing the juice from its thick stem between his strong claws. "The same thing that happened to the stem will happen to you!" he warned.

The young anteater was so brave that Brer Tiger wanted to run away. "Brer Fox," he said, "this animal is too small for me. You can have him."

Brer Fox slyly grinned, "Oh, Brer Tiger, why should I get scratched?"

"Coward!" shouted Brer Tiger. "I'll show you how to deal with him!" Brer Tiger stooped to kill, but the young anteater was ready. He dug his claws into the large beast's back. The forest shook with the tiger's cries.

"Save me, Brer Fox! I'm hurt!" Brer Tiger shouted.

Brer Fox leaped on the young anteater and began to bite him. The anteater hit Brer Fox and sent him twisting in pain to the ground. As soon as they could stand, poor Brer Fox and Brer Tiger fled.

Suddenly, both the tiger and the fox flew into the air. Each was hanging with a foot in a rope lasso. There they stayed, swinging and shouting. From behind some bushes came Brer Rabbit, who had helped the young anteater again. He had made the foot traps in which he caught both animals.

Brer Tiger and Brer Fox begged, "Set us free! Set us free!" Brer Rabbit agreed if they promised to go far, far away.

That night, the anteater, his family, Brer Rabbit and other forest friends had a great party with ice cream for everyone except the brave young anteater. Instead, he had a special treat—a big dish of red ants.

Weeds

BRER MAN WAS GROWING SUGAR CANE on his *fazenda* or plantation. He was a stingy fellow, and he wanted to get rid of the weeds that crowded his cane without paying for the work. Since his fields were full of mosquitoes, he had a problem until he thought of a plan.

At a special meeting of the animals, Brer Man promised, "I'll give a prize, Homero the ox, to the one who'll pull my weeds without scratching himself."

Brer Man thought to himself, "All the animals will try, but they'll all start to itch and scratch. I'll get the weeding done, and I won't have to give the prize. I'll show them who's smart!"

The first to try was Sis Jaguar. As she began to work, the wind sprayed her with sticky seeds. They caused her to scratch for the rest of the day.

Next, Brer Armadillo wanted a chance. Since he walks with his stomach close to the ground, he rubbed the thorny twigs which had fallen there. "I have to scratch my belly," he said. Of course, he also lost the contest.

Then came Brer Turtle. With his short legs, he scraped the dirt. In only a few minutes, he was scratching stickers that stuck to him.

Brer Monkey, who followed his friend, should have lasted longer. But he suffered from mosquito bites before pulling a single weed. He did a little scratching dance on the field, scratching from his toes to the top of his head and up each arm and leg.

After all the other animals tried, it was Brer Rabbit's turn. He

worked a while before he heard a mosquito buzz and land on his face. As if this were not enough, he felt he had to scratch the tip of his nose. He was just about to give in when he saw Brer Man watching. To make himself feel better, he leaned his nose against the end of the hoe for a moment.

Now he could go back to work. But soon the itching began to last so long, he thought he would scream. Brer Man believed he was winning. He asked, "Is something bothering you?"

Brer Rabbit quickly told him, "I wanted to ask you if Homero has a spot here." On the last word, the little one dug into his stomach for a moment right on the spot that was itching.

"No," said Brer Man, none the wiser. "What Homero has is a stripe that runs down his back. It's quite pretty."

"Oh!" cried Brer Rabbit. "A stripe down here?" As he asked, he scraped his claws with all his might from head to tail. He was rid of his itching!

Brer Rabbit worked without stopping for an hour. By the end of that time, he felt he just had to scratch the mosquito bites on the right side of his body.

Brer Man was looking closely at him. The rabbit called, "Listen, boss, they tell me Homero has an ugly bald spot right here." Brer Rabbit showed where by clawing the itching place on his right side.

Brer Man replied, "No, that's wrong. He's only bald on his right hip where someone hurt him."

"Here, boss? Or is it here?" Each time Brer Rabbit asked, he scraped with his claws where it itched most. In this way, Brer Rabbit worked without stopping until the job was finished. Of course, the labor of the other animals helped him.

When the weeding was finished, Brer Man announced, "Here, Brer Rabbit, I give you Homero the ox. You've earned him. You weeded that whole field without scratching. I know because I watched you."

Brer Rabbit tied vines around Homero's horns. He led him up the road, patting him on the leg. How proud the rabbit was when other animals cheered as he passed them with his prize!

The Corn

THE ANIMALS WERE FINDING IT HARD to hunt for food, so they planned to grow corn on a farm rented from Brer Man. He would be paid four carts of corn after they picked their crop.

Sis Cockroach, Brer Rooster, Sis Fox and Brer Wolf took the best land. Their fields had rich brown earth, perfect for corn. They gave Brer Rabbit rocky ground on the side of a hill. Everyone worked on the land except Brer Rabbit, who took one look at his field and never went back.

"I'm not a planter," Brer Rabbit told Brer Man. "I'd rather read books. My desk is my farm. In my swivel chair I can turn around or lean back and think. When I've thought too much, I can play my violin. Even though I won't be farming, I'll have plenty of corn. You'll see!"

Brer Man said to him, "You'll have to work like the others. If not, I'll bet that, by the end of the year, you'll starve."

Brer Rabbit quickly replied, "I'll agree to your bet. I won't waste my time or money. By the end of the year, though, I'll own all the corn I'll ever need. I'll show those animals who grabbed the best land for themselves. Let's shake on the bet." And they shook.

Time passed quickly and at the year's end, there was plenty of corn. After all the ears were picked, Brer Rabbit went to the home of Sis Cockroach. "I'll pay you if you bring me a cart of your corn," he offered. She was willing, naming the day and hour for delivery.

After that, Brer Rabbit said the same thing to Brer Rooster, then Sis Fox, and finally, Brer Wolf. Each was to come to his storehouse a half hour later than the one before. He made a pitcher of punch and bought some candy for the guests.

Sis Cockroach came on time on the right day in a cart loaded with corn. "Dump it quickly," Brer Rabbit told her. "Then come in

and drink some punch, Sis Cockroach. Your money is here waiting for you."

Sis Cockroach unloaded her corn and entered the house to enjoy the drink. Since she heard another cart not far away, she asked, "Er . . , er. . , who can that be?"

"That's Brer Rooster, who's bringing more corn," Brer Rabbit told her.

"Brer Rooster?" Sis Cockroach asked fearfully. "Give me my money! I don't want to be here with him."

"Your money is safe. There's no need to hurry," Brer Rabbit said. "Just hide under that big box. Brer Rooster won't know you're here." There was no time to leave, so she did as she was told.

Just then, there was a knock at the door. Brer Rooster called cheerfully, "I've brought your order, Brer Rabbit."

"Dump it in the storehouse," Brer Rabbit said. "Afterwards, come in for some punch. Your money is ready."

As Brer Rooster unloaded his cart, he saw some corn there already. When he went inside for his punch, he asked, "Who was here before me?"

"It was Sis Cockroach. She's already left," Brer Rabbit replied. He spoke in a loud voice, winking and pointing to the big box which hid her. Brer Rooster ate Sis Cockroach at once.

In the meantime, a noisy wagon was on the road. "Brer Rabbit, come get my corn!" Sis Fox shouted.

Brer Rooster was trapped. He begged, "Hide me, friend! I don't like Sis Fox." Brer Rabbit put him behind the door.

When Sis Fox came in the room, "absent-minded" Brer Rabbit closed the door. Sis Fox ate Brer Rooster in a minute.

Then another cart with Brer Wolf turned toward the house. Sis Fox knew she was in danger. With Brer Rabbit's help, she hid behind the long window curtains.

When Brer Wolf came in, Brer Rabbit said, "It's mighty stuffy in here. Please open the window."

As Brer Wolf drew near the window, he smelled Sis Fox behind the curtains. In a few moments, he had her in his teeth.

Just as Brer Wolf was ready for some candy, a fourth visitor faced the house. It was Brer Man with a gun. Brer Wolf ran under the bed in Brer Rabbit's room.

Brer Man told Brer Rabbit, "I was surprised to find your storehouse full of corn."

"Yes, you've lost your bet," Brer Rabbit said. "You didn't believe me before. From now on, maybe you will. My storehouse is filled with corn I didn't plant. Brer Wolf, who's under the bed in that room, can tell you I'm not lying."

Brer Man wasted no time. He went into the bedroom and killed Brer Wolf. "Brer Wolf always ate my cows. I'm glad to give him what he deserves," Brer Man explained. "I made a bet with you, Brer Rabbit, and lost. The truth is I don't feel so bad. At least I got Brer Wolf."

"Let's have some punch," Brer Rabbit said cheerfully. "I finally got even with the animals who took all the good land and left me a rocky hillside. I drink to your health, Brer Man, and the bet I just won!"

Brer Rabbit filled two glasses. Then he leaned back in his swivel chair and smiled.

The Tin Can

CAREFREE BRER RABBIT TOOK CHANCES with big animals just for the fun of it. One day, he was playing his violin near the top of a deep hole where he lived. When he heard Sis Jaguar's roar, he stopped playing at once.

Quickly Brer Rabbit made a trap in the middle of the road with thick vines. Then he brought the tip of the vines into his hole. Inside, he sat on the vine ends and waited, alert for every sound.

A second later, Sis Jaguar appeared. She was a queenly yellow beast with dark spots that looked like black velvet pasted on her back. She held her head high and never looked at the ground.

Sis Jaguar was prancing down the road when she put one of her front legs in the middle of the trap. Brer Rabbit was still, very still, while she placed both hind legs in the trap. Then he made the mistake of sighing. Sis Jaguar heard the noise and stopped. She was so angry she was foaming at the mouth. With great effort, she freed herself and leaped toward the vines. It was her hard luck to find the enemy hiding in a hole too small for her big body.

Brer Rabbit was laughing at her in his underground home. She could hear his voice, but she couldn't reach him. "I'll sit beside this hole," she thought. "He won't stay there for the rest of his life. When he comes out, I'll grab him and claw him to pieces!"

Sis Jaguar waited three days and three nights for Brer Rabbit. After that, she thought, "I might fall asleep, so I'll sit on the hole to be sure he can't get out." Her tail dangled in the hole.

Brer Rabbit saw something moving atop his hole. At first he thought it was a snake. He learned the truth just when his foot slipped on an old tin can, and he thought of a plan. He waited until the tail stopped swishing, a sign that Sis Jaguar was asleep. Quietly he used vines to tie the can to the end of her tail.

While Sis Jaguar slept, a small wasp made his way into her ear. The wasp slid its yellow-and-black body deeper and deeper into her ear. Sis Jaguar woke when she heard endless buzzing inside her head. She thought she would go crazy!

Sis Jaguar tried to scare the wasp by jumping high in the air. She fanned her tail from side to side against her body. The tin can on the tip of her tail struck her, first on her left ribs and then on her right leg.

"How did I get this can?" she asked. "Why did this happen now?"

She dragged her tail, hitting every rock in her path. Clink, clank, clink, clank! The loud noise made the wasp nervous. It began to sting inside Sis Jaguar's ear.

When Brer Rabbit heard Sis Jaguar's pained screams, he knew this was a good time to escape through the back of his hole. He left her at the front of his home, the wasp still buzzing and biting in her ear.

Wedding Party

SIS JAGUAR TOLD THE ANIMALS, "I'm going to get married."
Since the beasts were afraid of her, Brer Monkey whispered to them, "How can we get on her good side? I know —let's give her a wedding party!"

The animals thought, "We'll buy some peace. Now maybe Sis Jaguar will leave us alone for a while."

When almost everyone had agreed to a party, Brer Monkey suggested, "I'll be the speaker. I'll say something like this: 'Sis Jaguar is our Queen. Her coat seems like velvet. Her eyes sparkle. She is the strongest, bravest beast in the forest!'"

For his speech, Brer Monkey bought new reading glasses. To look his best, he ordered a short green dinner jacket with silk trimming.

When Brer Monkey began to collect money for a fancy dinner-dance, he came to see Brer Rabbit. Brer Monkey told him, "We know Sis Jaguar is mean. She chases us all the time. She's happy to make a meal out of someone in our family. Now she's going to marry, and it will be worse because she'll have cubs. There'll be more enemies to eat us."

"Then why are you giving her a party?" Brer Rabbit asked.

The monkey replied, "We're going to change her mood. When she remembers the food and the good things I say about her in my speech, she won't touch us anymore. You're a bright fellow. You can help."

Brer Rabbit answered, "Don't count on me! Do you think I'd stoop so low as to praise my biggest enemy? Just take my name off your list. I may be small, but I'm proud too!"

Brer Rabbit meant what he said. He turned to Brer Monkey to add, "You're the one who surprises me. You've read so many books. You know so much. Why do you give in to her?"

Brer Monkey's feelings were hurt, but he got over it quickly.

"Since you won't agree, don't ruin our plans," he told Brer Rabbit. "You like to get out of work. When there's a party, you always get there first. You let others pay while you enjoy free food and drinks! You take the best! At least say that you'll stay away from the party."

"I can't do that," Brer Rabbit replied. "If I weren't there, who would teach Sis Jaguar that there are still some honest souls? When the guests are all seated, I'll come quietly. I'll pull everything off the table and leave."

The monkey was so worried, Brer Rabbit told him, "Let Sis Jaguar know what I'm going to do. That way she won't blame you. And here's some news to cheer you: I won't eat there. Sis Jaguar and I don't like the same food anyway."

Brer Monkey shook his head sadly when he left Brer Rabbit. He sighed as he spoke to the bride about Brer Rabbit's plans.

"Relax! Don't be nervous, Brer Monkey," Sis Jaguar told him. "We'll trick him. He can't swim. We'll have our party on the island in the middle of the river. If he gets a ride, I'll handle him. We'll have one more dish at our feast—baked rabbit in tomato sauce. Relax! Leave that pest to me!"

Now it was the day of the party. Some last-minute jobs had to be done. Brer Monkey, swinging from a branch, tested his speech on the clouds above. Every time he repeated it, he flattered Sis Jaguar more.

In another part of the forest, Brer Lizard was busy. Since he was in charge of the party music, he picked sambas and bossa novas. "My silver horns will play carnival pieces. The music will make everyone think of Mardi Gras holiday dancing in costumes in the streets," he said proudly. "I'll polish my horns so they'll shine."

To get ready for the big event, Sis Jaguar took a long bath in a cool pool. Then she combed her sleek yellow and-black hair with her sharp claws.

When it was almost time for the party, the guests swam to the island. Those who could not get there alone were carried on the back of Brer Capybara, the water pig.

Brer Rabbit hid in the bushes and waited for everyone to cross. Then he sat on a large stone near the river bank. He was sad because he did not think he could keep his promise to Brer Monkey.

Brer Alligator also had been left out of the party. When he was swimming in the river, he saw Brer Rabbit's long face and drew closer. "Good evening," Brer Alligator said cheerfully. "Why didn't you go to the party?"

"How could I get there?" the rabbit asked. "I can't swim."

"Why I'll take you if you do something for me," the alligator offered. "Just bring me a piece of pork."

Brer Rabbit had a spark of hope now. "I do need a ride back

and forth, but we'd be taking chances," he told Brer Alligator. "The truth is, I've said I'll ruin Sis Jaguar's party. I've promised to pull the dishes off the table. If you take me, Brer Alligator, I'll throw the food to you. Then you'll get more than one piece of pork. You'll get the whole dinner!"

Brer Alligator could almost taste that food. Besides, he was angry because no one invited him to the party. Brer Alligator agreed to help, saying, "Climb on my back. We'll be on our way." Then he asked, "Brer Rabbit, are you afraid?"

"Afraid?" the rabbit replied. "If you knew me better, you would know that's not true. I want us to live 'til we're old, so I'm careful. If we leave here and go in a straight line, we'll be caught. Let's go to the other side of the island. There's less chance they'll see us. I'll meet you where the river turns."

The two had to keep out of sight. To meet his friend, Brer Alligator swam beneath the water.

Brer Rabbit remained unseen by hopping under the bushes. Before leaving, he rolled in sand and coated himself with dirt. You wouldn't believe how he looked! When he was on Brer Alligator's back, his fur was the same color as the muddy water.

Both friends landed safely on the side of the island away from the party. The noisy guests were drinking too much. Brer Opossum, for one, could not stand straight when he tried to dance the samba with Brer Monkey's squeaking daughter.

Brer Monkey himself was busy setting the table. He used a pretty white cloth with a fringe of long gold threads at the bottom. The flowers he put in the center were white orchids with purple throats. He served the national dish of cooked dark beans, pork, sweet potatoes and orange slices. On golden plates he put the hot food, and in tall, shining glasses, he poured apple-flavored soft drink, *guaraná*. He arranged small cups, ready to be filled with thick black coffee.

Brer Monkey clapped his hands to announce, "Dinner is served." He thought he was mighty important when he led Sis Jaguar to her place at the head of the table. "You may sit now," the haughty bride told the guests.

By this time, Brer Rabbit had reached the shore. Hungry Brer

Alligator stayed in the water. The rabbit crept silently near the party table and hid behind a tree trunk to calm himself.

Brer Rabbit reached with one arm until he got a firm grip on the tablecloth fringe. Then he pulled with all his might! Every bit of the food fell into the water. Brer Alligator's open mouth was waiting for it!

The animals were stunned. Brer Rabbit did not waste time. He jumped on the back of Brer Alligator and headed home.

When angry Sis Jaguar and the others caught their breaths, they looked toward the water. Brer Rabbit was in the middle of the river. "So long, see you again!" he shouted as he waved to them.

The Fountain

DURING A BAD DRY PERIOD, grouchy Sis Jaguar, Queen of the Beasts, told the animals, "You have to build a fountain where we can store rain water. If you don't work, you can't drink the water!"

The animals started at once to build a cement floor and high walls to hold every drop of rain. While they worked, Sis Jaguar rested.

Queen Jaguar yelled, "Brer Sloth and Sis Snail, you're too slow. You've got to move faster. All of you, push yourselves! This job should have been done by now!"

The animals mixed the cement in the blazing sun while Queen Jaguar stayed in the shade. Sis Butterfly's wings fanned the air around the Queen. The jaguar drank apple-flavored soda, *guaraná*, but she would not let anyone else have a sip.

Brer Rabbit looked at Sis Jaguar. He said, "Hm, I'll follow her example." He dumped his bricks and stopped working.

Brer Rabbit thought to himself, "I'm tired of Sis Jaguar's orders. I'll help if she asks in a polite way and, above all, if she works too."

When the fountain was built, Sis Jaguar punished Brer Rabbit by naming a guard each day to keep him from drinking the water. As time passed, the thirsty rabbit thought of a plan to trick the watchman at the fountain.

Brer Rabbit took the dried, hollowed shell of a gourd. He filled it with honey and put it in a safe place near the fountain. Under a nearby bench, he put a rope he might need. Then he played a tune on his violin for Brer Fox, the guard on duty.

Brer Fox asked, "Have you come to visit? You can't have any water, you know."

Brer Rabbit cried, "Well, Brer Fox, I want only a tiny drink. I'm dying of thirst."

"No, not here," Brer Fox replied firmly. "You should have done more work on the fountain if you wanted to use it."

Brer Rabbit knew he would not win this way. He put down his violin and brought over his gourd instead. "Brer Fox, my friend, stretch out your paw," he said. "Taste something I brought you."

Brer Fox dipped his paw into the gourd. He licked the honey on his claws. "It's so sweet!" he shouted. "But I want more than a little bit!"

Brer Rabbit told him, "Then reach with both your paws."

Greedy Brer Fox jammed both paws into the small opening in the gourd. They stuck there. Brer Rabbit got his rope and tied Brer Fox to a tree. Then he hopped into the fountain.

"Listen, Brer Fox," the rabbit explained, "I don't only want to drink the water. I also want to take a bath."

Brer Rabbit splashed in the water. He cooled his throat as he gulped whole mouthfuls. When he had drunk enough, he jumped out and waved goodbye to Brer Fox, who was tied to the tree. Then the rabbit played his violin all the way home.

After a while, Brer Billy Goat found Brer Fox and freed him.

Brer Billy Goat frowned. He tugged at his beard and scolded, "You let Brer Rabbit trick you!"

Soon Sis Jaguar stopped keeping guards at the fountain because Brer Rabbit was smarter than all of them. And ever after, the little rabbit drank water just as often as he wished.

Magic

BRER MAN AND THE ANIMALS feared and hated Sis Jaguar. They secretly laughed together at her mistakes. Her feelings were hurt most when Brer Lion was made King of the Beasts, because she thought she should be the ruler.

Brer Lion said, "Sis Jaguar tells lies about me. She has to stop being so high and mighty. Brer Rabbit, my spies will let you know where she is each hour. Please keep her away from the rest of us. Will you do this?"

"Gladly, very gladly!" Brer Rabbit replied. He clapped his paws at the thought.

After some time had passed, the animal world had a party for Brer Rabbit. Sis Turtle announced, "I give this medal to you, Brer Rabbit, for unselfish service. Since you keep Sis Jaguar busy, we can breathe easily."

Brer Anteater added, "Thanks to you, Brer Rabbit, we've enjoyed a good life. Even Brer Sloth has been free to go for walks. He always used to play it safe by sleeping in a tree day and night."

The party was in full swing, but Brer Rabbit left early. He suspected Sis Jaguar might come, and that is exactly what she did.

To lead his enemy away from the group, Brer Rabbit began to run. He stopped when he got thirsty. It was at a lake with water so clear he could see the sandy bottom. Beside the lake, Brer Rabbit found the body of a deer, dead about three days.

The sight of the deer was sickening, but its odor was even worse. Only Sis Jackal and her family hovered nearby. When the wind carried the odor south, all the flowers on that side wilted. It was just as bad when the whiff was carried north, toward the lake. The water formed ripples that crashed over rocks, trying to escape.

Brer Rabbit came near the dead deer. He said, "I'll pinch my nose. I'll breathe through my mouth." Quickly he removed the deerskin with a bamboo knife.

The skin was in the rabbit's hands when he heard the roar of Sis Jaguar, for she was following him. Brer Rabbit whispered, "There's no time to run and no safe hiding place. I'll cover myself with this deerskin."

Sis Jaguar faced an animal that did not walk straight. "What's wrong, Brer Deer?" she asked. "Not long ago, you looked fine. Now you seem dried up."

The smell bothered Sis Jaguar so much, she turned her head. Then she added, "Why don't you take a bath in the lake? If you don't, Brer Vulture may come for you. That bird likes the dead, and frankly, you smell more dead than alive."

The animal replied, "Nothing can be done about my smell. I had a fight with Brer Rabbit. He worked his magic on me. I felt my whole body shake. My mouth had a bad taste. My skin began to wrinkle. My bones started to rattle inside me."

The "deer" spoke sadly at first and then became more outgoing. He said, "I'm glad I ran into you, Sis Jaguar. You may already know something about his magic. We've both learned the hard way that it's best to leave Brer Rabbit alone. If not, his evil eyes will hurt us."

The wilted deer could hardly walk away. Sis Jaguar, who believed in magic, was very worried. She moaned, "Pity me for my past fights with Brer Rabbit! I'm going to be good to him now, but pity me for the past!"

When the jaguar could no longer see him, Brer Rabbit shed the deerskin. He had to bathe each morning for a week to get rid of its odor. "It was worth the trouble," he thought, "if the magic lasts."

The Moon

JUST BEFORE NIGHTFALL, Brer Rabbit did a favor for Brer Man. Brer Man was bringing home balls of cheese he had not sold at the market. The balls were always wrapped in green banana leaves, but by sunset the leaves were all dried out.

Brer Rabbit offered to help Brer Man. He said, "Wait here 'til I bring you more green leaves. They'll keep your cheese fresh." This was no sooner said than done.

Brer Man told his helper, "Here are two balls of cheese. It's my way of saying thanks."

With the cheese in his pocket, Brer Rabbit went to a distant river. By then the moon was high in the sky. It was a fine full moon which reflected clearly in the still river. "Oh, it's so pretty, and there's light enough for me to do some night fishing," Brer Rabbit said to himself, as he began to hum.

Brer Rabbit took out his fishing pole and threw in his line. He was too busy catching fish to be aware of Brer Tiger sneaking behind him. That big beast clutched the rabbit's ribs. He warned, "I'm going to dig my teeth into you, Brer Rabbit, ears and all!"

"Relax, relax," Brer Rabbit told him. The rabbit pretended not to worry, while he tasted one ball of cheese. "Before you eat me, have my other cheese ball. It's the best I've ever had!" Brer Rabbit gushed as he presented his gift.

Brer Tiger bit into the tasty cheese. "This is great!" he shouted. "Where did you get it? I want more."

"These two balls came from the bottom of the river. It's full of cheese down there," the rabbit said with a straight face. He pointed to the reflection of the full moon in the river. Innocently he asked, "Can't you see that creamy round ball shining in the middle of the water?"

Since Brer Tiger knew the animals feared him, he thought

they would not have the nerve to lie to him. He believed everything he was told. "That golden circle of cheese on the water is close," the tiger said. "I can almost reach it from the bank."

"That's where you're wrong," Brer Rabbit replied. "It looks close but it's not. It's at the very bottom of the river."

"Too bad, too bad!" Brer Tiger moaned. "I can never sink to the bottom. Tell me how you did it. You're so much lighter than I am." Just then, Brer Tiger looked at the rocks on the river bank. "If I could only get you to tie these rocks to my feet!" he said. "What could we use to hold them?"

Brer Rabbit pulled vines from a nearby tree. Brer Tiger cried, "Of course, vines are what we need. Listen, I don't think these stones on the river bank are big enough. Help me push two heavy rocks to the water's edge."

Brer Rabbit threw down his fishing pole so he could help. Together they pushed the rocks. Still panting, Brer Rabbit tied the rocks to the tiger's feet with five tight layers of vines.

When all was ready, Brer Tiger shouted, "Push me into the water!" As he sank gently, he reached for the reflection of the moon that he thought was cheese. It disappeared. He hit the rocky bottom with not one sign—not even a speck—of cheese in sight.

The water current was so strong, it carried Brer Tiger to a shallow spot. The tiger gasped for breath. He sputtered, "You lied to me. No one dares do that! I'm not even sure you were really fishing. What kind of fish could you catch this late at night?"

Brer Rabbit raced up the river bank shouting, "Sucker fish!"

Fish and Syrup

BRER TIGER AND BRER FIREFLY went fishing and threw everything they caught into the same basket. The fishermen were enjoying so much success, they did not want to quit. They stayed longer than they planned, stopping only when it was dark. Since clouds hid the moon now, the only light came from Brer Firefly's glow.

Brer Tiger said, "It's time to divide the fish. I'm larger than you. I'll take all the large fish. You're small. I'll give you one small fish for each of mine." That made Brer Firefly so angry, he put out his light.

Poor Brer Tiger had to stumble home in the dark carrying his heavy basket of fish. He dropped it in front of his door and went inside to rest.

At the same time, Brer Firefly told Brer Rabbit how the tiger kept all the big fish they caught together. To get even, Brer Rabbit hid with his son outside Brer Tiger's house.

Brer Rabbit said to his child, "Go tell Brer Tiger he can have a quarter of the pig I've just killed. I'll even give him spices he and his wife can use when they cook it."

Brer Tiger smiled at the fine offer. Tired as he was, he walked slowly up the long road to Brer Rabbit's house. Meanwhile, Brer Rabbit grabbed Brer Tiger's basket of fish. He hid it and took the short cut home.

Brer Tiger knocked at Brer Rabbit's door. The rabbit opened it with tears in his eyes. He cried, "My pig's been stolen! My pig's been stolen!"

Disgusted, Brer Tiger sighed and went home. Then Brer Rabbit fried the big fish. As he ate a tasty meal with his son, Brer Rabbit thought, "The person who enjoys the fruit of the garden may not be the one who plants it."

Brer Tiger stomped up and down when he saw his fish were

gone, guessing who took them. He had no time to worry about this because the next day, his wife, Sis Tiger, gave birth to four chubby babies. Brer Tiger was so proud to be a father, he ran all the way to Brer Rabbit's home, forgetting about the night before.

The new father announced, "I want you to be the godfather, Brer Rabbit. You can name the children. For this special event, I've bought a whole barrel of syrup. I've put it in my shed. I have to hunt now, but I'll be home tonight. Then we'll have a party!"

Sis Tiger was surprised at odd times during that same day. Brer Rabbit would knock on her front door and suggest a name.

"Call the first child Begun," he said.

Later he added, "Name the second child Half-gone."

When he knocked a third time, he suggested, "Name the third child Finished."

After the fourth knock, Brer Rabbit told her, "Call the last child Upside Down." Then he stumbled home with a swollen stomach.

When she went to the shed, Sis Tiger understood the unusual names Brer Rabbit gave her children. That night, she showed her husband the empty syrup barrel, and he cried because he had been so stupid.

"Last night and again today, that rabbit rascal has made me pay for his greed! When will I ever learn?" Brer Tiger asked through his tears.

The Wind Storm

IT WAS THE HOTTEST TIME of the year, and the sun was blazing when Brer Rabbit hopped under his favorite mango tree. He liked to eat the sweet, juicy, yellow-orange fruit clinging to the big hard seed. He dozed in the shade of this tree, but his nap ended when Brer Tiger grabbed him.

The tiger said, "It's lucky I have a rope with me. I'm going to tie you and hold you for my supper!"

Brer Rabbit opened one eye lazily to whisper, "It's you I feel sorry for, not me."

"Why?" Brer Tiger wanted to know.

"Because I won't be around. You'll be caught in a wind storm," Brer Rabbit answered. "It's going to pass this way any moment."

Brer Tiger was afraid of such storms, and Brer Rabbit sensed it. "Are you sure?" the tiger questioned.

"Of course!" Brer Rabbit told him. "The sudden heat is a sure sign. I don't care, because I won't be here long."

"Forget about you. I'm more worried about me," Brer Tiger said. "How can I make myself safe?"

Brer Rabbit replied, "I'll use your rope to tie you to my tree. It has never been uprooted by storms in the past. There's a good chance it will hold up through this one. Now, even if the wind is strong, you won't blow away."

Brer Tiger begged Brer Rabbit to tie him right away. The tiger lay still. He wanted the rope put on tightly. When Brer Rabbit finished, he hid himself atop the mango tree, just to watch. He enjoyed his prank so much his nose twitched.

The first to pass that way was Sis Calf. She laughed as she asked Brer Tiger, "Why are you, such a big beast, tied with a rope?"

"I'm going to save myself in the big wind storm," Brer Tiger said. He was proud that he was prepared.

"What storm?" Sis Calf wanted to know.

48

"The one everyone's talking about," Brer Tiger replied.

"I've just come from town," Sis Calf said. "I didn't hear one word about a storm." She grinned and shook her tail as she hurried away.

Brer Tiger gritted his teeth. He said, "Oh, I'm so hungry for calf steak! Why did I allow Brer Rabbit to trick me? I'll ask the next animal I see to untie me."

Soon Brer Monkey appeared. The monkey jumped over Brer Tiger.

"Please untie me," Brer Tiger begged.

"If I do, will you promise not to eat me?" Brer Monkey asked.

"I promise. I promise," Brer Tiger said.

Brer Monkey stooped to bite the ropes. As soon as Brer Tiger could move, he seized the monkey. "I'll swallow you even though you freed me!" the tiger cried.

Brer Rabbit, safe in the mango tree, saw what was happening. He told Brer Tiger, "That's not the way to eat Brer Monkey. Toss him high in the air. Open your mouth wide. He'll be juicier when he lands."

Brer Tiger liked this fancy idea. He leaned against the mango trunk and tossed Brer Monkey high in the air. In fact, he tossed him so high, Brer Monkey grabbed the branch of the tree and scampered out of sight.

What landed in Brer Tiger's open mouth was a mango seed thrown by Brer Rabbit. Brer Tiger coughed as he spit out the seed. He growled to Brer Rabbit, "Some storm! You're nothing but a tiny bag of hot air. You'd be the first to blow away in a real wind storm!"

Brer Lion and Sis Turtle

ONE EVENING AS THE SUN WENT DOWN, tired Brer Rabbit was making his way through the bushes. He had been chased by other animals for many nights. "I need a resting place," he sighed.

Brer Rabbit came upon the foot of a young tree that had grown joined to the trunk of an old one. "Between these trees is a perfect bed of dry leaves," he observed. "It's in this hollow ditch between the roots. I've looked all around and can't see any danger in staying."

Brer Rabbit yawned. "No one will notice me," he said. "I'll cover myself with leaves the same color as my body. It will be great to just shut my eyes."

Soon Brer Rabbit fell into a deep sleep. His nostrils barely moved when he breathed.

A short time later, Brer Lion was looking for a place where he could nap. He saw a cozy spot near two trees and threw his heavy body down. He never even knew that tiny Brer Rabbit was under him.

Luckily, Brer Rabbit was not hurt. He was lying between two roots that protected him. When he felt the load atop him, Brer Rabbit thought, "I can hardly breathe. I'll have to think fast to get out alive!"

Brer Rabbit decided to scare Brer Lion and escape. He shouted, "WHO IS STEPPING ON MY FINGER?"

The King of the Beasts sat up. He placed his paw on Brer Rabbit's stomach. He muttered, "Hmmm! If what I'm touching is only a finger, who knows what the size of his hand is like! I better get out of here before this monster eats me!"

With his tail between his legs, Brer Lion ran as fast as he could. Never once did he look back.

Brer Rabbit still needed his sleep, but he heard his friend, Sis Turtle. She was crying, "Help! Help!"

Sis Grinny Granny Fox had caught Sis Turtle and put her in a sack. The fox mumbled, "I'm going to take her straight home. On my way, I'll think about my best turtle recipes. Let's see, should I bake, broil, or fry her?"

Brer Rabbit was angry. He thought, "I eat only vegetables. It's cruel to kill animals for food. Poor Sis Turtle! I have to save her!"

Brer Rabbit rose from his bed of leaves and went to a tree that had a beehive. "I'll cut this branch carefully. I dare not bother the bees," he muttered. "I'll wrap leaves tightly around the hive and put the branch with the hive ever so gently in my sack."

Brer Rabbit rushed with his sack to Sis Grinny Granny Fox's house to wait for her return. As she came up the path, Brer Rabbit yelled, "You got here just in time. At the back of your house, chickens are digging in your garden. They're ruining your plants."

Sis Grinny Granny Fox threw down her sack. She ran to her garden and never once looked back.

Brer Rabbit freed Sis Turtle from the fox's sack. He warned, "Hurry! I'm putting the beehive in your place. We'll leave her sack on the ground, but we'll hide to see what happens." How the rabbit loved a prank!

Sis Grinny Granny Fox returned, frowning. "That Brer Rabbit is no good," she moaned. "Lucky for him, I can't find him now!"

The Fox took her sack to the kitchen. She put it on a bench near her stove and said, "Sis Turtle, don't beg for your life!"

When Sis Grinny Granny Fox opened her sack, was she surprised! Hundreds of angry, starving, stinging bees flew toward her!

Brer Rabbit and Sis Turtle saw everything through the window. Satisfied, they told each other, "Come on, let's go home."

As they left, Sis Turtle whispered, "Since Sis Grinny Granny Fox can't have turtle steak, she should try eating bee soup."

Sly Brer Rabbit laughed, "Who's doing the eating?"

The Wax Doll

ONE SUNNY DAY, SIS GRANDMOTHER bought a big watermelon. "It's so sweet and juicy," she said, "I'll plant its seeds in neat rows on my farm."

Every morning and evening, Sis Grandmother watered those seeds until they sprouted. Then she got down on her bony knees. She weeded the young plants and put rich brown soil around them.

Thanks to her care, the vines became thick and strong. In no time at all, there were flowers, and later, fruit. Sis Grandmother was very excited. She went to town — a long trip — to tell everyone about her fine watermelons.

The doctor asked, "May I buy one?"

"You may have the largest one when it's ready," Sis Grandmother promised him.

The grandmother chose a special melon for the doctor. She gave it extra water and waited for it to ripen fully. She did not know Brer Rabbit had his eyes on the very same fruit.

But one night, Brer Rabbit hopped into her garden. He made a small hole in that watermelon and ate a bit. He came back every night for more, making sure to cover the hole every time. Sis Grandmother's eyesight was pretty poor, so she never noticed what was happening to the good doctor's melon.

Soon there was only an empty watermelon shell clinging to the vine. Brer Rabbit filled the shell with dirt and covered the hole. The fruit still seemed heavy.

The next day, Sis Grandmother thought, "My special melon is beginning to turn yellow. I'll pick it and carry it to the doctor. My goodness, it's heavy! I'll just shift its weight on my back."

The good doctor was pleased with the melon. He paid Sis Grandmother at once. "It's so big," he told her, "it might be extra sweet."

At dinner when the doctor cut the melon, his face fell. He couldn't speak. Dirt spilled over the snowy white tablecloth. His wife screamed! His children giggled!

"Oh, am I angry!" the doctor cried. "I'm going to see Sis Grandmother at once!"

When he got to her farm, he shouted, "What a dirty trick you pulled!"

Sis Grandmother was surprised. "I couldn't do such a thing," she said to him, "but I'll find out who did." Then she gave the doctor a new watermelon. "I won't rest 'til I know the name of the rascal!" she promised.

Sis Grandmother hurried to the watermelon patch. She lifted leaves and looked. Soon she found small paw prints in the dirt. "Aha, Brer Rabbit was my visitor," she said. "He must also be the one stealing eggs from my hen house. I'll set traps for him."

The thief took the eggs when it was dark, so Sis Grandmother watched night after night to catch him. Her house had two porches, and several trees were on her lawn. In the moonlight, she climbed to the upper porch where the trees hid her. She carried her gun, shooting at every noise. That was a mistake, of course, because it made Brer Rabbit keep out of sight.

"Shooting him is not the answer," she decided. "I'll try something else."

The next morning, Sis Grandmother was busy. "I'll get some tree sap," she thought. "I'll mix sap and wax from beehives to make a sticky doll." She paused and asked, "What will make her look real? Oh, I know. I'll dress her in my old clothes."

Sis Grandmother placed the dressed doll between the watermelon patch and the hen house. "Something more is needed," she said to herself. "I'll put a slice of my cornbread in one of the doll's hands and cheese in the other. Aside from his big ears, Brer Rabbit is mainly stomach. He loves cornbread with cheese."

She stepped back to see the effect and muttered, "I better bend one of the doll's hands towards its mouth. It really looks like a lady eating." Sis Grandmother grinned and her eyes sparkled as she went back to her house singing, "I'm sure I'll catch Brer Rabbit now!"

Brer Rabbit was no fool, but he was fond of food. When he came in front of the wax lady, he could hardly believe what he saw. He thought, "Ahh, cornbread with melted butter on top! It smells so good!"

The rabbit asked the doll, "Will you give me your cornbread and cheese? If you don't, I'll punch you!"

The doll said nothing, of course. Brer Rabbit became angry. He gave her a very hard blow. "Hey, my paw's stuck in your neck!" he said.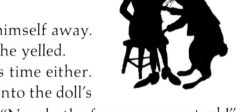

Brer Rabbit tried to pull himself away. "Let me go or I'll hit you again!" he yelled.

There was no answer this time either. Brer Rabbit threw his other fist into the doll's

 sticky body. "Now both of my paws are stuck!" he shouted.

"Listen, either you give me some cheese and cornbread or I'll kick you!" Brer Rabbit cried. He kicked with one hind paw, then the other. "Both my hind paws are stuck!" he screamed.

He thought he could get the best of her somehow. "One butt in the jaw and you're done!" he told her. Brer Rabbit reared back his head and let it land on the jaw of the wax lady.

"Ay, my head's stuck!" he moaned.

The rabbit still wanted the cheese and cornbread. "I'll hit her with my belly," he said. "It'll be my last try."

Now, all night long, his whole body was stuck to the wax doll. "How terrible!" he sighed.

At sunrise, Sis Grandmother went to see if anyone had tried to get the cornbread and cheese. She laughed so hard, her stomach hurt. "At last I've caught you, Mr. Melon Head," she gloated, clapping her hands. "I'm going to stew you!"

Sis Grandmother grabbed Brer Rabbit. She shook him free from the wax doll and threw him under a box. "I'll boil some water. Then I'll let my tomatoes and onions simmer," she told him as she went to her kitchen. Brer Rabbit knew he was in trouble!

Soon Brer Fox passed. He heard cries for help and saw the upside-down box. "Who's making such a fuss here?" he asked.

"That's Brer Fox," the rabbit said to himself. "Brer Rabbit is under this box," he said aloud. "Sis Grandmother put me here for stealing a watermelon. She's getting even with me."

Brer Rabbit added, "She's bringing me a chicken and says I must eat it. But I can't put animals in my mouth. You know that, Brer Fox, but she doesn't. I get sick at the thought of a fat chicken."

Brer Fox's mouth watered. "I want that chicken," he thought. He asked Brer Rabbit, "Would you like me to take your place? God made your mouth small to eat carrots. But chicken, that's for me! Why don't we switch?"

"I'll let you take my place, Brer Fox. It's only because we're such good friends," Brer Rabbit told him. "With others, I'd have thought twice about it. Get me out of here, please, and I'll help you in!"

Foolish Brer Fox took the box off Brer Rabbit before getting under it himself. "How lucky I am!" he said. No sooner was the fox inside, though, than Brer Rabbit began to put big stones atop the box.

"What're you doing, Brer Rabbit?" Brer Fox asked.

"I'm piling stones on the box the way Sis Grandmother left it," Brer Rabbit answered. "When I tried to get out, I moved the rocks. They fell off."

"Oh, in that case, add as many as you can," Brer Fox replied. "I want her to find everything as she left it. Poor old lady!"

Brer Rabbit placed bigger and bigger stones on top, though none had been there before. He thought, "I'll make sure Brer Fox can't get away. I think I'll stick around to hear what Sis Grandmother says. That should be funny!" He eagerly hid and waited.

Cheerful Sis Grandmother was whistling when she returned. "Hmmm, I don't remember any rocks on top of the box," she said as she removed them. "But my memory's slipping a bit."

"It's been a long time since I've had rabbit stew," she sang. Then she said, "I believe I'll add some celery to make it perfect."

Sis Grandmother removed the box and grabbed the trapped animal. "What is this?" she asked. "My rabbit's become a fox!"

As she carried the fox to her kitchen stove, Sis Grandmother mumbled, "Is my eyesight really that bad? I better get new glasses."

Behind a tree, Brer Rabbit listened. He whispered, "It's so easy to fool dear Sis Grandmother. Hmmm, I better not test my luck any longer!"

Brer Rabbit went to the river to remove his sticky coating, a reminder of the wax doll. While bathing, he heard the cries of Brer Fox.

The fox was yelling, "Ay! You're putting me in boiling water. Oh, that rabbit! If I get out alive, I won't leave one hair on his body!"

The Fair Judge

A T SUNRISE, BRER MAN said to himself, "I'll pick these reeds for my baskets." Then he paused to ask, "What's that I hear? It's coming from under the tree uprooted in last night's storm."

Sis Snake was screaming, "Lift the tree. Save me! Save me!"

Brer Man took the time to free the slithering creature. "How do you feel?" he questioned her with concern.

"I'm fine. This small belly sore is all I have to remind me of that awful night."

Mean Sis Snake did not thank Brer Man. Instead, she told him with a sneer, "You've saved my life. Now, to pay you for the favor, I'll bite you to death!"

"How can you do this?" the kind man wanted to know. "Are you going to repay good with evil? Pity me; don't kill me! Let's go to the King of the Beasts. He'll be our judge."

"To Brer Lion?" replied Sis Snake. "No, indeed, I won't go before His Bushy-tailed Majesty! It would be better for us to walk together and ask the first three animals we meet. We'll do what two of the three say. Do you agree? If not, I'll bite you now!"

"I agree," the scared man answered. "There's a little hope for me this way."

The two walked until they saw Brer Ox chewing his food in a pen. Near the pen was a slaughterhouse where animals are killed for their meat. Sis Snake and Brer Man told the ox what had happened. "Who is right, Brer Man or me?" Sis Snake asked.

Brer Ox replied, "I say Sis Snake is right. Men use us when we're strong. They get rid of us after we're weak. When I was young, I helped a farmer cut through the hard ground with his plow, so he could plant seeds. While he plowed, he made me wear a heavy wooden collar, a yoke around my neck. It cut me and hurt all day long."

Brer Ox touched his neck where it was still sore. Then he added, "In those days, the farmer took care of me because I pulled his plow. Now that I'm old and can't work, he's sent me to be killed. You must know how I feel! Sis Snake, get even with all men by biting this one!"

Brer Ox had spoken from the heart. Now he turned to shake the flies off his back.

Sad Brer Man kept walking with Sis Snake. Next, the two met Brer Horse in a field with soap plants. Brer Man thought, "If I can get away from Sis Snake, I'll dig the roots of those plants and use them to wash my dirty body. They'll be my soap. But Sis Snake watches me every minute."

Sure enough, Sis Snake was always within striking distance of Brer Man as she flattered Brer Horse. She said, "How lucky we are to find such a bright creature! You can tell Brer Man and me what to do." She explained the problem and waited for his reply.

"I'll never vote for any man," Brer Horse grumbled. "Men have claimed I'm their best friend. Then they've jumped on my back. They've made me pull big wagons loaded to the top. When I was frisky, I carried them and their heavy bags everywhere. In return, I was treated well."

Brer Horse cried as he thought of "the good old days." He told his visitors, "As years passed, I slowed down. Men began to hit me and let me starve. You can see, Sis Snake, I want you to bite Brer Man."

Brer Horse said, "Goodbye." Then he scratched himself against the soap plants.

"Listen, Brer Man," scolded Sis Snake, "two have already voted against you. We'll only talk to one more. It looks bad for you!"

Brer Man's head hung low as they looked for the third animal. After a while, they met Brer Rabbit. He seemed to be waiting for them in a bamboo field.

"Hello," Brer Rabbit greeted them. "It's strange seeing both of you together. You look worried, Brer Man. You're smiling, Sis Snake. What's happened?"

Sis Snake told the story without giving the answers of Brer

Ox and Brer Horse. "Just reply whether you're with me or against me," she told Brer Rabbit.

"Do you want me to be fair?" Brer Rabbit asked.

"Yes," both replied at the same time.

Brer Rabbit spoke softly. "Because this is so important, I have to see the place where it began. I want to know what you were doing, Sis Snake, when Brer Man saved you. Does that make sense, friends?"

The two agreed, so all three went back to the fallen tree. Brer Rabbit looked around him. He told Brer Man, "Please lift the tree." He said to Sis Snake, "Please place yourself as you were the night before." Since both wanted a fair answer from Brer Rabbit, they did what they were told.

Brer Rabbit leaned toward Sis Snake. "Can you get out of there alone?" he wanted to know.

"No, no, I can't," Sis Snake told him, beginning to feel some of her old fear.

Then Brer Rabbit spoke to Brer Man. "Take that branch at your feet. Hit Sis Snake on the head! Kill her! Don't be foolish!" he said.

"Why have you taken my side, Brer Rabbit, when no one else did?" Brer Man asked.

"Because you've been my friend. You've planted carrots," the rabbit answered. "Please show your thanks by not setting traps for me."

After Brer Man agreed, the rabbit kept urging him, "Go ahead, use that branch like a club. Give Sis Snake a blow and have her for lunch!"

And that's exactly what Brer Man did. But the rabbit knew Brer Man might not be friendly for long. "I myself could be served at one of his meals," he thought.

So Brer Rabbit ran away, his fur tail bouncing high in the air.

Bibliography

The Brer Rabbit stories in this book are retold. The ideas for them are in these folktale collections:

Jaramillo Arango, Euclides. *Los cuentos del pícaro tío conejo.* Bogotá, Colombia: Banco Cafetero, 1961.

Lisboa, Henriqueta. *Literatura Oral para a Infancia e a Juventude.* Rio de Janeiro, Brasil: International Board of Books for Young People, 1968.

Parsons, Elsie Worthington (ed.). *Journal of American Folklore,* XXVI, parts 1-3. Boston, Massachusetts: American Folklore Society, 1936.

Rivero Oramas, Rafael. *El mundo de tío conejo, cuentos populares venezolanos para niños.* Caracas, Venezuela: Ministerio de Educación, 1973.

de Salles, Franklin. *Coelho Sabido.* São Paulo, Brasil: Ediçoes Melhoramentos, 1967.

_____. *A Volta do Coelho Sabido.* São Paulo, Brasil: Ediçoes Melhoramentos, 1967.

Thank You Notes

I thank the Temple University Research and Study Leaves Committee, whose travel grant made it possible for me to collect some stories; George H. Weiss, Argentina Palacios and Barbara Holdridge, who edited; student Crittendon Harris, who did early work on some translations; author Muriel Feelings, who read the introduction; and both Carolyn W. Field and Helen Mae Mullen of The Free Library of Philadelphia, who encouraged me.

I especially thank my aunt, Sylvia Corona, of Mexico City, who helped me learn Spanish, and my deceased mother, Yetta Nelson, who united me with relatives in Argentina on my first trip to South America thirty-six years ago.

DR. JAQUELINE SHACHTER WEISS, an associate professor for fourteen years at Temple University in Philadelphia, Pennsylvania, where she taught children's literature, took early retirement to pursue her special interests in this field. In 1974 and 1977 she collected Brer Rabbit stories while leading studytours in children's literature to the Caribbean islands and South America. She is currently the moderator/distributor of "Profiles in Literature," ongoing videotaped interviews with leading children's book creators, seen by over 100,000 viewers internationally. She is also the author of *Prizewinning Books for Children*, published by D.C. Heath, and together with Carolyn W. Field, *Values in Selected Children's Books of Fiction and Fantasy*. Her home is in Pennsylvania.

Photograph by Robert Curtis

CLINTON ARROWOOD started out not as an artist but a flutist, after studies at the Peabody Institute in Baltimo: A habit of making sketches in the margins of his music to posters for Peabody concerts, formal art training, history courses, a prize-winning record album cover, fil strips and the three books for which he has achieved far along with author Donald Elliott: *Alligators and Mu. Frogs and the Ballet* and *Lamb's Tales from Great Operas.* work has been featured as well in the *New Yorker, Time. other magazines. In addition to his art assignments, Cl ton Arrowood teaches music appreciation and art histc at Garrison Forest School in Owings Mills, Maryland, a still performs as a free-lance flutist from time to tin *Young Brer Rabbit* represents the artist's first foray ir full-color book illustration.

Designed by Barbara Holdridge
Composed by Brown Composition, Inc., Baltimore,
    Maryland, in Palatino
Printed on 86-pound acid-free White A Matte coated
    paper and bound by Everbest Printing Company,
    Hong Kong/Four Colour Imports, Ltd., Louisville,
    Kentucky